The Spirit Made Me Do It
Poetry Made Spiritually

Donald T. Williams

authorHOUSE®

AuthorHouse™
1663 Liberty Drive
Bloomington, IN 47403
www.authorhouse.com
Phone: 1-800-839-8640

First published by AuthorHouse 9/14/2011

ISBN: 978-1-4634-4861-5 (sc)
ISBN: 978-1-4634-4860-8 (hc)
ISBN: 978-1-4634-4859-2 (e)

Library of Congress Control Number: 2011915061

Printed in the United States of America

Dedication

This book is dedicated with love and gratitude to my grandmother, grandfather, mother, father, siblings, aunts, uncle, nieces, nephew, cousins, and especially to my Aunt Juanita, Uncle Nelson and the wonderful people of Mount Calvary Baptist Church, located in Brooklyn, N.Y. 11233. I love you all.

Acknowledgements

There are several people, who have been part of my personal and professional life, to whom I am deeply indebted and could cite in a lengthy list of acknowledgements. Of course, the members of my nuclear and extended family have, in some form or fashion, contributed to this literary work, as have several former students, parents, colleagues, and superiors in over thirty years of service with the New York City Department of Education. More like family and friends, countless students, parents, and coworkers have had faith and stood by me when I questioned my personal value, professional worth, convictions, and self respect. You, all of you, remain in my memory and heart. It is pointless to name you individually because you already know who you are and how I cherish the fleeting time spent with you . I am forever grateful to have been associated and of service to you.

I would also like to thank the City College of New York, the New School for Social Research in New York City, and Wesleyan University of Middletown, Connecticut for welcoming and supporting my undergraduate and graduate studies so many years ago. Please, after being most patient or perhaps giving up on collecting anything of merit from me in our lifetimes, won't you receive this humble, but sincere, return on your investment ? I pray that I have not disappointed you.

Finally, but of course, truly first, I would like to thank God the Father, Jesus Christ, the Holy Spirit, and several TV Ministers and Pastors who dutifully preach and teach the gospel of God's Word in Richmond, Virginia and other cities throughout America and around the world as well. Your sacred efforts and messages are reaching and saving souls even more then you can think or incredibly imagine. I will bear witness and testimony to this. Sincerely, thank you and may God continue to bless you and me.

Introduction

From my early years to beyond middle age, I never was a very religious person. Respectful of my mother's beliefs, wishes, love for God, and the church, I attended, but was always in conflict with what was being presented for acceptance and obedience. First, there was my failure to comply with two of the Commandments by becoming an accomplished thief and liar at a young age. Second, I imagined the pastor as the Devil with reddened face, horns, swinging tail, and pitchfork in the pulpit one terrifying Sunday. So vivid was the image, the resulting nightmares haunted my dreams for months and ruined church for me. Kids are so impressionable, you know. Now, skeptical of the fervent preaching, singing, shouting, fainting, and so forth, I convinced myself I could never cut it as a Christian and opted to be a "good sinner" with ethics rather than an outright hypocrite, if there's a difference.

While all of this church conflict was developing, my incredible father was supplying plenty of impressionable data and know-how on how to be a "man", but not necessarily a Christian. Eat, look good, dress well, make money, work hard, tinker, drive fast, tell other people what to do, smoke, drink, gamble, come and go when you want, show love sparingly during the year but graciously on vacations and holidays, and cuss randomly as fitting or gratuitously when angered. My dad—what was not to love and admire? For me, it was as simple as monkey see, monkey do. And besides, he never went to church and seemed pretty content with his lot. Live, love, die, and let the chips fall where they may. It's all a crap shoot, and my daddy loved craps but worshipped poker, his revolver, and the thick bankroll in his pocket. Me, I preferred Blackjack, out suckering the long odds of the slots, big bills in a money clip and semi-automatics, but you get the idea.

Life continued past those formative years. Good and bad choices were made as I navigated the middle ground of my world and society. Suited in a stylish neutral shade of morality grey and a "winner" in just about everything I ever did or prayed for, I considered myself blessed and charmed. "God still loves me. The Devil can't touch me." Or so I thought. Fast forward past forty-five years of sex, drugs, rock n roll, college, marriage, career, the occult, children, involuntary commitment, quasi separation, quasi reconciliation, retirement, sex, drugs, rock n roll, a second, bonafide separation, more involuntary commitments, betrayal, wrongful incarceration, rip offs, divorce (?), and God to today. Something significant and unexpected occurred as I meandered through life along the middle ground while singing my tune, "Donnie can't lose. Do as I choose." Like a thief in the night, like successive Nazi lightning bolts on a clear, cloudless sky, the thunder clapped, and boom! Trapped, I crapped out, crapped my pants, was treated like crap, and felt like crap too! Without exaggeration or doubt, when this happens to you, it's a life changing experience. No…! And, "You Only Live Twice", Mr. Don.

I had lost it all and found mental illness and homelessness in the Dirty South. Literally and figuratively, in one fell swoop, everything I loved and worked for was disavowed. Like a double agent in an action packed psychological thriller, I was burned, disowned, and faced with a mission possible. Against all odds I had to forget about the ghostly "if onlys" haunting my mind and concentrate on survival and self-preservation. Back against the wall of a 23 and 1 lockdown cell, I did what many brothers do with time on their hands under similar circumstances. Miraculously and conveniently, I found Jesus in a Bible I stole and began to read earnestly. Well, maybe I didn't steal it; somebody left it, and I took ownership of it in my desperation. In a 23 and 1 lockdown, you'd better have something to read. I prayed, read, and reached out to an old friend I hadn't knelt for and spoken to consistently and sincerely for years. Now that I was out of my comfort zone and sought Him, I wondered if He'd hold it against me for dissing Him and cavorting with the Devil so blatantly. What if He hears prayers in the order in which they come in and always, always takes His time in answering them? Let's face it. He is God. And what comes around, goes around. Ratts! Fortunately for me, and I don't know how to put this any other way than to say, God must have a soft spot for basket cases and rock n roll rodents. Praise the Lord!

The poems of this book are a compilation of voices in my head. They are the thoughts, current beliefs, emotions, and spiritual sensations which formed and emerged from a broken heart and mind being attended and mended by the Holy Spirit's touch. Reading the Bible for the first time and hearing the voice of God as I did had a healing impact on my life. This I truly know and believe. Talk about mysterious ways! In the famous words of the God Father of Soul, "Good God! I got that feeling!" People obviously react differently when touched by the Holy Spirit, and you are holding my reaction in your hands. It is my prayer that what I've received in the Spirit is as contagious as a Christian pandemic, and that the Holy Spirit's infectious power of love passes to, through, and from me to you until the entire world succumbs to God's undeniable Truth. Did I just hear you sneeze? Well then, "Yes you! Bless you!" Now sanitize and start reading. That's a joke, but I mean it. Bless you!

Table of Contents

~ Food for Our Souls ~

Donald T. Williams

Jesus
Jesus

Jesus is food
For our souls

Jesus
Feed us

Doing God's will
Is our goal

Some people hunger for diamonds
Some people hunger for gold

Some people hunger for things of the flesh
They don't care where their soul goes

Jesus
Jesus

Jesus is food
For our souls

Feed us
Jesus

Doing God's will
Is our goal

Some people hunger for power
Some people hunger for fame

Some people hunger for nothing at all
They should make wisdom their aim

Jesus
Jesus

Jesus is food
For our souls

Feed us
Jesus

Doing God's will
Is our goal

Some people hunger for diamonds
Some people hunger for gold

Some people hunger for things of the flesh
They don't care where their soul goes

Jesus
Jesus

Jesus is food
For our souls

Feed us
Jesus

Doing God's will
Is our goal

Doing God's will
Is our goal

~ *Praise My God* ~
Donald T. Williams

I praise my God
Hear what I say
I praise my God
Each time I pray

I praise my God
Both work and play
I pray my God
Shows me the way

I praise my God
Thy kingdom come
I praise my God
The only one

For what He's done
For what He'll do
And if you're thankful
You'll praise Him too!

Come love my God
There is no shame
Come love my God
His Holy name

Come love His Son
Who bore our pain
Come love His life
Death not in vain

I praise my God
For all I have
I praise my God
Keeps my heart glad

I praise my God
Come good or bad
I praise my God
And don't get mad

I praise my God
Please do the same
I praise my Lord
Who bore no blame

Poured out His blood
On Calvary
Lamb sacrificed
On wicked tree

Come love my God
There is no shame
Come love my God
His Holy name

Come love Jesus
He bore our pain
Come love His life
Death overcame

I praise my God
Through thick and thin
I praise my God
Draw, lose, or win

For what He's done
For what He'll do
And if you're thankful
You'll praise Him too!

I praise my God
Both night and day
I praise my God
Both work and play

I praise my God
Hear what I say
I pray my God
Shows me the way

~ This Guy ~
Donald T. Williams

This Guy has no limits
This Guy has no bounds
This Guy walks on water
And His steps make Holy Ground

This Guy heads the pasture
His Father is the Boss
This Guy paid my debt for me
And His Daddy bore the loss

Yes, He is my Jesus
Lord is Prince of Peace
Trust Him when I'm wide awake
Trust Him when I'm sleep

My Jesus is my Savior
So meek, so mild, so kind
My Jesus is my teacher
Healer of the blind

This Guy's coming to Earth
Having died and rose again
Revelation tells us,
But we can't say when

Best that you be ready
Best you stay on guard
This Guy will defeat the Devil
And He won't spare the rod

This Guy has no limits
This Guy has no bounds
This Guy walks on water
And His steps make Holy Ground

This Guy heads the pasture
His Father is the Boss
This Guy paid my debt for me
And His Daddy bore the loss

This Guy feeds the hungry
This Guy finds the lost
This Guy turns green everything
From pine trees down to moss

This Guy has no limits
This Guy has no bounds
This Guy walks on water
And His steps make Holy Ground

This Guy heads the pasture
His Father is the Boss
This Guy paid my debt for me
And His Daddy bore the loss

~ Abba Daddy ~

Donald T. Williams

You,
Hold me in your arms
Snuggled nice and warm

I'll never be too grown
Not to call you Daddy

You,
Keep me safe from harm
Sheltered in the storm

I'll never be too grown
Not to call you Daddy

Abba is your name
And Father is the same

My Abba Daddy does
Everything with love

Set me on your lap
Let's just sit and chat

I'll never be too grown
Not to call you Daddy

Abba is your name
And Father is the same

My Abba Daddy does
Everything with love

Take your foot and tap
Rock me until I nap

I'll never be too grown
Not to call you Daddy

Abba Daddy do
All that you can do

To help your children see
God is all they need

Hold me in your arms
Keep me safe and warm

I'll never be too grown
Not to call you Daddy

~ Meek and Mild ~

Donald T. Williams

I'll be meek and mild
Just like a child
For you

I'll be careful
In the things
I say and do

There's no problem
In obeying
All your rules

And I know that come
What may
You'll see me through

Thou art my God,
My Lord,
My Prince of the Pasture

You give me hope
To keep the faith
When faced with disaster

I know that come what may
You'll find a way
To see me through

I'll be meek and mild
Just like a child
For you

I'll be careful
In the things
I say and do

There's no problem
In obeying
All your rules

For the Word
As you have written
Is all true

Thou art my God,
My Lord,
My Prince of the Pasture

You give me hope
To keep my faith
When faced with disaster

Come what may
I know
You'll see me through

And I'll be meek and mild
Just like a child
For you

~ Who Knows? ~
Donald T. Williams

Who knows the number
Of leaves on a tree?

Who knows the number
Of breaths in me ?

Who sees my each
and every thought?

Who makes me thirst
And want for naught?

'Tis the one who fills the wishing well
'Tis the one to whom my secrets tell

'Tis the one who speaks the cricket's tongue
'Tis the one who knows the battle's won

Who knows my dreams
Before I sleep?

Who gives the Word
And vows to keep?

Who fills my heart
With endless joy?

Who loves me
Like His only boy?

He is my God
The one and only

He is my God
Who's Wholly Holy

He is my God
On whom I depend

He is my God
My Father and friend

~ It's All True ~

Donald T. Williams

It's all true
And I know I believe
I can't be fooled
And I won't be deceived

Night turns to day
On the clock
Twenty four seven

Sure as He was born
There's a home for me
In Heaven

Lord, set my feet
On the Rock of Solid Ground
Lord, let my ears
Hear each note the trumpet sounds

When the Roll is called
And the names are revealed
My soul be saved
My fate was sealed

Because I believed
That it's all true
By God's great grace
Somehow, I knew

He gave His life
And died for me
My faith is based
In what I can't see

Thank God I can read
His Word in the Book

Thank God I was baptized
And the cleansing took

So glad the world
Now hears my heart sing!

I'm blessed with true love,
The King's of Kings

It's all true
And I know I believe

I can't be fooled
And I won't be deceived

~ There Is ~

Donald T. Williams

There is a time
There is a place

Where life won't end
When judgment's faced

A bride and groom
Will soon be wed

Two will be one
As vows are said

Will you be scared
Or unprepared?

Did you not heed
Through thought and deed?

The Son of God
Gave you the chance

To sit it out
Or rise and dance

Jesus, I'm yours
And you are mine

We are like grapes
From the same vine

You shed your blood
For love of me

And I am yours
Eternally

There is a time
There is a place

Where life won't end
When judgment's faced

Don't be scared
Be prepared

Be sure to heed
In thoughts and deed

~ Just Read His Words ~
Donald T. Williams

Just read His Words
As they are written
And just like me
You'll be quite smitten

Head over heels
You'll surely feel
His matchless love
All your life through

What you must do
To know the truth
Is just read His Words
As they are written

Just read His Words
As they are written
And just like me
You'll find them fitting

Hold them as dear
Music to ears
Kept in your mind
Today for all time

Just read His Words
A song like the birds
As they were given
As they were written

His love abounds
With every sound
Of His sweet voice
You soon will hear

Just read His Words,
A song like the birds',
As they are given
As they are written

Just read His words
As they are written
And just like me
There'll be no quitting

Through trials and tears
He'll draw you near
Lay burdens down
And give you a crown

Just read His words,
A song like the birds',
As they are given
As they are written

Just read His words
As they are written
And just like me
You'll be quite smitten

Head over heels
You'll surely feel
His matchless love
All your life through

What you must do
To know the truth
Is just read His Words
As they are written

~ Lord Lift Me Up ~
Donald T. Williams

Lord lift me up
In these troubled times
Throw me a rope
Drop me a line

From places on high
Look down on me
Like what I do
Like what you see

Lord lift me up
In these troubled times
Help me hang tough
Keep my heart kind

Lord lift me up
From the depths of despair
I am your child,
And I know you care

Tides rise and fall,
But it's all your call
So long, long ago
You made it so

Lord lift me up
From a pond like a duck
Let me fly high
As the birds of the sky

Lord lift me up
In these troubled times
My life is yours
And things will be fine

Lord lift me up
In these troubled times
Throw me a rope
Drop me a line

From places on high
Look down on me
Like what I do
Like what you see

Lord lift me up
In these troubled times
Help me hang tough
Keep my heart kind

Lord lift me up
Give my heart wings,
A spirit that soars
A voice that will sing

Sing songs of love
And praises for you
When I feel sad
Or if I feel blue

Lord lift me up
In these troubled times
My life is yours
And things will be fine

~ Pay Your Tithes ~
Donald T. Williams

Pay your tithes
To the Lord
Ensure your room
Ensure your board

In His House
Way on High
There you'll dwell
If you try

At His table
Is your seat
Loved ones wait
To meet and greet

Pay your tithes
To the Lord
Fill His storehouse's
Open doors

Say your prayers
Both day and night
Do what's good
Do what's right

Heed His Word
In thought and deeds
Let His Love
Meet all your needs

Pay your tithes
To the Lord
Stay in His Word
For its reward

His Kingdom's yours
If that's what you seek
His Words are as true
As a promise He keeps

Pay your tithes
To the Lord
May your wealth
And blessings soar

There's no way
You can pay
Or try to buy
A place on High

To rob my God
Can't be good
Best you pay your tithes
Like you should

In His House
You will reside
Reservations
Made through tithes

Pay your tithes
To the Lord
Ensure your room
Ensure your board

There you'll dwell
If you try
In His House
Way on High

~ A Cross ~

Donald T. Williams

I wear a Cross
Around my neck
It is a symbol
Of my respect

Respect for You
Respect that's due
For all You gave
For souls You have saved

I wear a Cross
Around my neck
It is a symbol
Of my respect

I wear a Cross
Around my neck
I live my life
As You'd expect

With a heart full of love
And arms that will hug
A wretch just like me
Hung on the next tree

When all seems lost
I clinch my Cross
And whisper a prayer
Broadcast through the air,

Lord, comfort me
Calm stormy seas
Have all I do
Be of honor to You
God, spare them
Pain and misery
Forgive
What they have done to me

I wear a Cross
Around my neck
It is a symbol
Of my respect

Respect for You
Respect that's due
For all You gave
For souls You have saved

I wear a Cross
Around my neck
I live my life
As You'd expect

~ Wedding Day ~

Donald T. Williams

My life was in shambles
All dreams were deferred
The road was so bumpy,
And my vision was blurred

I was running on empty
The very last in my class
I was grasping at straws
'Til there were no straws to grasp

So, I cried out your name
And confessed what I shamed
A foul life full of sins
Committed time and again

But, my Lord brought me back,
And I cleaned up my act
As if in a dream,
I was washed 'til I gleamed

Reborn and brand new
A lovely creature in You
The mighty Lord is my life
We live like husband and wife

There'll never be
A divorce
Our love has
An endless source

Make this
"Your lovely wedding day"
May you find Christ;
I hope and pray

~ Save Me My Lord ~

Donald T. Williams

Save me my Lord
From an endless death
Breathe into me
The Holy Spirit's breath

Save me my Lord
From man's discord
Please give to me
Sweet Harmony

Sweet Harmony
In voice and song
Sweet Harmony
Both rich and strong

Christ gave His life
Without regret
Now all mankind
Is in His debt

Throughout this world
Should be one rule
That we will love
And not be cruel

Save me my Lord
From an endless death
Breathe into me
The Holy Spirit's breathe

Save me my Lord
From man's discord
Please give to me
Sweet Harmony

May I sing
A simple song
Praising good
Condemning wrong?

May I sing
A simple song
Praising God
All the day long?

Christ gave His life
Without regret
Now all mankind
Is in His debt

Throughout this world
Should be one rule
That we will love
And not be cruel

Save me my Lord
From man's discord
And give to me
Sweet Harmony

Sweet Harmony
In voice and song
Sweet Harmony
Both rich and strong

May I sing
A simple song
Praising good
Condemning wrong?

May I sing
A simple song
Praising God
All the day long?

~ All Praise To Thee ~

Donald T. Williams

So unique as snowflakes
Falling from the sky
Universal mystery
Apple of Newton's eye

Galileo's daydream
Dickens' Tiny Tim
All of these are possible
I know because of Him

Phantom of the Opera
Phantoms of the sea
Sweetness of the honeycomb
And the stingers of the bees

All of these are possible
Thanks is due to Him
This is why we have the Psalms
And sing our Holy Hymns

Our blessings are so bountiful
Throughout our world we see
Bow your heads in gratitude
And say, "All praise to Thee"

All praise to Thee
I give my God
All praise
I give to Thee

So thankful
For the seed you gave
The root
And the fruity tree

~ *It's With* ~

Donald T. Williams

It's with fortitude
I cling to you
It's with gratitude
I sing to You

In humility
I kneel to You
All hostility
I yield to You

As a lamb
That nourishes on sod
Or a angler
Reeling in a cod

I am yours
You are God
On this Earth,
I'm blessed to trod

Blessed to have You
With me in my corner
Blessed to have You
During this life's sojourner

Blessed to have You
In times thick or thin
Blessed to have You
All about and within

In humility
I kneel to you
In gratitude
I sing to you

You are my fortitude
You are my strength
Ever present
Our distance linked

By the sunlight
And starlight bright
You guide my way
Both day and night

It's with Your love
I've learned to give back
My heart so filled
I never lack

It's with gratitude
I sing to You
All hostility
I yield to you

Blessed to have You
In my corner
Blessed to have You
During this life's sojourner

~ Precious Moments ~

Donald T. Williams

Precious moments with my Lord
All alone behind closed doors
Never lonely, never bored
He and I of one accord

Can you hear the angels sing?
Feel the fluttering of wings?
Yes, the time is drawing near
The Lord's Day will soon be here

Precious moments with my God
Joined together in a crowd
Singing songs of praise in mass
Sharing thoughts in Bible class

There's no place I'd rather be
Everywhere He's here with me
Yes, the time is drawing near
The Lord's Day will soon be here

Precious moments with my Lord
All alone behind closed doors
Never lonely, never bored
He and I of one accord

Can you hear the angels sing?
Feel the fluttering of wings?
Yes, the time is drawing near
The Lord's Day will soon be here

Can you see the mount with Three
Hanging from those hurtful trees?
Comes the special One of them
On His Word we can depend

Can you hear the angels sing?
Feel the fluttering of wings?
Yes, the time is drawing near
The Lord's Day will soon be here

Precious moments with my Lord
All alone behind closed doors
Never lonely, never bored
He and I of one accord

~ Thank You ~

Donald T. Williams

Walking with me
By my side
Always with me
Every stride

Watching over
As I sleep
Drying tears
When I weep

Thank you, God
For whom You are
Father of
The Son they scarred

Thank you, Lord
For sparing me
The heavy load
And cruelty

What can I do
In return?
Read your Word
And speak what's learned

Preach and teach
So all will know
You're my God
Who loves me so!

Loves me so
Both good and bad!
Loves me so
And I'm so glad!

Walking with us
By our side
Always with us
Every stride

Watching over
As we sleep
Drying tears
When we weep

What can we do
In return?
Share your Word
And spread what's learned

Thank you God
For whom You are
Father of
The Son they scarred

Thank you, Lord
For sparing us
Thank you, God
In whom we trust

~ He ~

Donald T. Williams

Who can count the seconds
Or calculate the sun's days?
Notice every movement
And make the waves behave?

Knows if there are aliens
Long within our midst
Knows who we have hated
Although our lips have kissed

Keeper of all secrets,
Mysteries, riddles, and the like
Owner of the Twilight Zone
Who aluminates the night

Call Him anything you want
Or call Him not at all
He's the reason you can think
Your thoughts both big and small

Master of the Universe
The beginning and the end
Genesis to the Revelation
Chapter and verse, the Word from Him

~ The Last Stand ~

Donald T. Williams

We are but clay
And putty in Your hands
We are but seeds
Cast all about Your land

So many are we
As countless as the sand
We are the faithful breed
Who obey Ten Commands

We are the lambs
For whom, Your pasture grows
We are the sparrows
In Your sight below

So many are we
As countless as the sand
We are God's valiant soldiers
Making the Last Stand

Side by side,
We form a mighty band
Singing hymns
And praying hand in hand

If you doubt our numbers
Or if our hearts are true,
Underestimating your opponent
Spells defeat for you

We are lambs
For whom, God's pastures grow
Jesus Christ, our Shepherd
How He loves us so!

Now are the days
Christain ranks fall in
We'll forge ahead
Like driven sandstorm wind

We are but shaped putty
In Your tender, loving hands
We are but seeds given a chance
To live by Ten Commands

If you doubt our numbers
Or if our hearts are true
Underestimating your opponent
Spells defeat for you

So many are we
As countless as the sand
We are God's valiant soldiers
Making the Last Stand

~ Minding My Business ~
Donald T. Williams

Minding my business
Is the best thing I do
Keeping my nose clean
Is high up there too!

Yes, I love my neighbor
And give respect as it's due
Prepared as a Boy Scout (Girl Scout)
On his (her) Ps and Qs

Ever so watchful
I dot I's and cross T's
I make sure Old Satan
Can't get over on me

On bended knee
I spend time in prayer,
Spend time in church
And pay tithes there

Of one thing, I'm certain
Just as prophets foresee
Jesus is returning
I'm as sure as I can be

Yes! my Father's children
Sure as whales swim the seas
There will be great fire
In Victory guaranteed!

Minding our business
May mean minding yours
Helping out our neighbors
And opening our doors

Loving and trusting
Helps to set us free
Making us true Christians
The kind we strive to be

Minding my business
Is the best thing I do
Keeping my nose clean
Is high up there too!

Of one thing, I'm certain
Just as prophets foresee
Jesus is returning
I'm as sure as I can be

~ Make No Mistake ~

Donald T. Williams

Make no mistake
About whose side you're on
Side with the Father
Side with the Son

Fools don't know
The Battle's already won
Think life's a joke
Think it's all fun

Live for today
Without caution or care
Whose days are numbered?
There are more days to spare

Are you the one much wiser
In how you live your days?
Trying to solve life's mysteries
As you travel through its maze

Make no mistake in choosing
Just who you should be with
The choice is "Oh" so simple
If you choose to live

Live a life eternal
Beyond all space and time
Sign up with the winners
Holy Trinity most Divine

~ Give Back ~

Donald T. Williams

Give back those gifts
He gave to you
Spend them with thrift
And pay levies due

Waste not Want not
Is the rule
Give back those gifts
Let His Glory shine through

Open closed doors
Give back what's yours
You're so unique
Rise to your peak

You've got a dream
Top it with cream
You're the "cherry" to boot
Atop huge triple scoops

If you are adrift
Without focus or aim,
Redeem your gifts
You know, the ones with your name

The ones with your genes
The ones with your schemes
The ones with your plans
Be you woman or man

Give back those gifts
Because it's right
Give back those gifts
With all your might

Give back those gifts
Lay them in plain sight
Give back those gifts
For His delight

Waste not, Want not
Is the rule
Give back your gifts
His Glory in you

~ A Servant's Spirit ~

Donald T. Williams

A servant's spirit
Serves Him so well
So many blessings
See how they swell

Always keep giving
To those in need
A servant's spirit
Bestows good deeds

While sharing
Our precious time
Showing our love
And being kind,

A servant's spirit
Somehow compels
To trust in Him
And all is well

Nursing the ill
Doing thy will
Clothing a child
Stir up a smile

Teaching the young,
Look what you've done!
Share what you have
With those who have none

So many blessings
See how they swell
A servant's spirit
Serves Him so well

~ Six Words ~

Donald T. Williams

Faith is what sustains us
When our troubles we can't bare

Love is what surrounds us
When we fear that no one cares

Truth is all that matters
When it comes down to it all

God is who stands for us
Even when we trip and fall

Wisdom is a fine treasure
Store it up for it's so rare

Understanding is a blessing
Those with love and wisdom hope to share

These six words are so abstract
Intangible some say

For Christians they are concrete,
Tangible as night and day

~ When ~

Donald T. Williams

When I'm feeling all alone
When no one calls on the phone
When the children are all grown
When my house is not a home

There's a comfort that I seek
I indulge in a sweet treat
No confection or baked cake
It's God's Word that I partake

Yes, I just sit down and read,
And the Good Word plants a seed
A seed in my heart that grows
Sprouts spring to my head and toes

Nourishing my every need
Seems I'm feeding as I read
I'm a flower
I'm a weed
Mustard seeds make mighty trees!

I'm the grape grown on the vine
And my nectar tastes just fine
God, He fills my very soul
I feel so complete and whole

~ The DND ~

Donald T. Williams

The Devil's in the details,
In the fine print no one can read
Loopholes so smartly worded
In tiny language that conceals

Comes the King of Counselors
Supreme Justice of the highest degree
One and only Friend in Court
Whose Gospel is decree

He exposes Satan's lies with truth
Deftly, deadly, details are revealed
Vision to Blind Justice is restored
As crippled clerks click their healed heels

The Devil's in the details,
In the fine print no one can read
Loopholes so smartly worded
In tiny language that conceals

Comes the King of Counselors
Supreme Justice of the highest degree
One and only Friend in Court
Whose Gospel is decree

Highest Court so lofty
Day of Judgment still unknown
All will stand before Him
God Almighty on the Throne

~ *Oh, How He Loves Me!* ~

Donald T. Williams

Oh, how He loves me
And lights my soul!
Oh, how I love Him
From whom life flows!

There is no other
I care to know
His gracious mercy,
Kindness bestowed

Reigning forever
Before time began
He is the Giver
With open hands

What we must know
And understand
He is the One God
Supreme and Grand

Twisters that spin
Hurricane winds
Blizzards of snow
Sandstorms that blow

Displays of power
In His control
His to contain
His to let go

Oh, how He loves me
And lights my soul!
Oh, how I love Him
From whom life flows!

Reigning forever
Before time began
He is the Giver
With open hands

Cascades of wonder
Subtle and bold
God's wrath or mercy
Ours to behold

Displays of power
In His control
His to contain
His to let go

Hurricane winds
Sandstorms that blow
Twisters that spin
Blizzards of snow

What we must know
And understand
He is the One God
Supreme and Grand

Oh, how He loves me
And lights my soul!
Oh, how I love Him
From whom life flows!

Cascades of wonder
Subtle or bold
God's wrath or mercy
Ours to behold

~ Never Give Up ~
Donald T. Williams

Never give up
On God or you
Believe what God says
His Words are true

Determination to do
Actions that succeed
His promise is yours
Through tenacity

Times may be tough
Things may be hard
Never give up
On you or God

Never give up
On God or you
Believe what God says
His Words are true

P.S. Thank you Joyce Meyers

~ The Holy Spirit ~
Donald T. Williams

As winds of change are blowing
As seeds we cast are sowing

Comes a reaping of like nature
Comes our one and only Savior

Calling God's army to attention
Time's for intervention

Lightning's flash crack claps of thunder
Angels sing and it's a wonder

Ten Commands of His I keep
Friend or foe my love I keep

I house the power
Of the Holy Ghost

My body's His temple
My heart is His host

Supernatural is so natural for me
No human boundaries for my capabilities

No Hocus Pocus magic
No Charlatan's trickery

I'm one Holy Spirit spectacle
For all the world to see

Does it sound as if I'm boastful?
Does an air of conceit rise from me?

All hail the Holy Spirit
As it permeates the breeze!

All hail the Holy Spirit
As I pray on bended knee!

All hail the Holy Spirit
And the good it does through me!

As winds of change are blowing
As seeds we cast are sowing

Comes a reaping of like nature
Comes our one and only Savior

All hail the Holy Spirit
As it permeates the breeze!

All hail the Holy Spirit
As I pray on bended knee!

All hail the Holy Spirit
And the good it does through me!

~ It's Up To You ~

Donald T. Williams

It's up to you
To choose to believe
It's better to give
Than to receive

The choice is yours
Be it blessings or grief
Your choices in life
Create the fabric you weave

You may or may not be
Cut from the same cloth,
But you're a textile of God
Made with lamb's wool so soft

It's up to you
To choose to believe
The righteousness of Christ
Is your identity

You can choose to be wise
Or act like a clown
All smiles today
Tomorrow all frowns

You choose to be loud
Or not make a sound
Remember what comes
Will go around

The choice is ours
Be it blessings or grief
Our choices in life
Create the fabric we weave

We may or may not be
Cut from the same cloths,
But we're a textile of Almighty God
Clothed in the Lamb's wool so soft

It's up to us
To choose to believe
The righteousness of Jesus
Is our identity

It's up to us
To believe He was crowned
That Jesus rose up
And He'll come down

It's up to you
To choose to believe
It's better to give
Than to receive

The choice is yours
Be it blessings or grief
Your choices in life
Create the fabric you weave

~ Seeds of Faith ~
Donald T. Williams

Live by Faith
In good times and in bad
Maintain your confidence
God's Word keeps our hearts glad

The human spirit is a field
In which different seeds are sown
Seeds of faith find fertile soil
Unbelief seeds are also sown

Take care which you plant
In your only heart so dear
Daily read the Word of God
Daily feed your spirit cheer

Have principles
To live by
The Book of Proverbs
Tells us them
In verse

Keen ears
Hear His Word
Tongues speak
Minds rehearse

Feed the Word into your spirit
Shine a light on what's not true
Enemies of faith surround us
As the cares of the world do

Religious traditions
Can cause misdirection
Men's Philosophies
Can misconstrue

The human spirit
Is like a field
What you plant
Is up to you

Unbelief is a bad seed
In need of soil to grow
That which contradicts God's Word
Threatens your very soul

You must tend the field of your heart
Rid your heart of unbelief
Protect your faith and never yield
To the thief of your beliefs

The human spirit is like a field
What you plant is up to you
Planting faith seeds is what to do
Almighty God will see your harvest through

Come into the Promise of God
A Promise Land is prepared for you
Plant faith seeds throughout your life
Reap the crop of truth

P. S. Thank you Pastor Randy Gilbert

~ Have You Not Read? ~

Donald T. Williams

Have you not read?
The Scriptures God gave?
Do you not know
How you should behave?

Has He not said?
All that you must do?
Think of Him first
That is the first rule

God wrote Ten Commandments
With His finger in stone
Moses, the Law Giver,
Made sure God's Will was known

You are to obey
With no questions asked
God would not command you
An impossible task

You have the will
Each one and all
To do no ill
Have mercy for all

Fill loving cups
And drink to no end
Never give up
On foes or friends

Have you not read?
The scriptures God gave?
Do you not know
How you should behave?

Has he not said?
All that you must do?
Think of Him first
That is the first rule

We are to obey
With no questions asked
God would not command us
An impossible task

We have the will
Each one and all
To do no ill
Have mercy for all

Fill loving cups
And drink to no end
Never give up
On foes or friends

Have you not read?
The Scriptures God gave?
Do you not know
How you should behave?

~ *God's Love Sustains Me* ~

Donald T. Williams

Lord, have mercy on my soul
It's more precious than pure gold
Help me live life free from sin
Fight the "good fight" to the end

God's love sustains me
Jesus has claimed me

Idol or lover
I'll have no other

Light my way and direct me
Up the path to victory
There's but one goal in my heart
To please Him once my day starts

God's love sustains me
Jesus has claimed me

Idol or lover
I'll have no other

Holy Spirit in my heart
Live in me and don't depart
Give keen sight so I can see
My eternal destiny

God's love sustains me
Jesus has claimed me
I'll have no other
Idol or lover

Life may have its mysteries
Days gone by are history
What's ahead is all that counts
And His bloodshed on the Mount

God's love sustains me
Jesus has claimed me

I'll have no other
Idol or lover

Lord, have mercy on my soul
It's more precious than pure gold
Help me live life free of sin
Fight the "good fight" to the end

~ The Glory of God ~

Donald T. Williams

The Glory of God
Is majestic to see
Just open your eyes
Survey your surroundings

There are details so small
In His mountains so tall
Some too minute
For the bare eye to see,
Yet, they are there as plain as can be

All along the sandy shore
Submerged on the ocean's floor
Live the wonders of the deep
Dream of them when you're asleep

In the skies above so blue
Rainbows bend and show their hues
Walk down any city street
People of His world you'll meet

Elephant
Or tiny flea
Each
Are of His majesty

Solar Systems
Cinema Stars
Light bugs
Caught in jelly jars

His creations large and small
Those with names or none at all
Things that just the blind can see
Things not of reality

The Glory of God
Is majestic to see
Just open your mind
Survey your surroundings

Tapeworms in your gut below
Sharing every bite you swallow
The mighty Mississippi's meandering flow
Alexander Graham Bell's invention's ring tone

Roasted peanuts
Lug nuts and screws
Hybrid cars
And canned cashews

His creations large and small
Those with names or none at all
Things that just the blind can see
Things not of reality

The Glory of God
Is majestic to see
Just open your mind's eye
Survey your surroundings

~ Not One Day Goes By ~

Donald T. Williams

Not one day goes by
I don't set out and try
My best to reach you, Lord
I always seek you, Lord

And since you died for me,
It seems my destiny
To lift my voice and sing
Your Father's King of Kings

Lord lift me up so high
Give my heart wings that fly
A spirit that adores
A holy life that's yours

My will is strong and I
Will love you until I die
And face you eye to eye
Before your Throne so high

Take me
Please make me
Humble
But not mumble

When I speak of you
Have done and will do
Blessings and mercies
Drink for the thirsty

Shape me
Please mold me
Hold me
Console me

In times of trouble
Or pins burst my bubble

Not one day goes by
I don't set out and try
My best to reach you, Lord
I always seek you, Lord

And since you died for me,
It seems my destiny
To lift my voice and sing
Your Father's King of Kings

My will is strong and I
Will love you until I die
And face you eye to eye
Before your Throne so high

Lord lift me up so high
Give my heart wings that fly
A spirit that adores
A holy life that's yours

Not one day goes by
I don't set out and try
My best to reach you, Lord
I always seek you, Lord

~ *If You Forgive* ~

Donald T. Williams

If you forgive
And choose to live
Like a wholesome host
Of the Holy Ghost

Things you once did
You no longer do
Tiger stripes change
A new creature are you

It's wise to give in
The Devil can't win
God knows how you've been
He's seen all your sins

If you forgive
And choose to live
A life of peace
Blessings increase

Take things in stride
Let Him inside
Good things will start
Open your heart

You now walk in the light
What was dark is now bright
God will keep you in sight
What He sees brings delight

It's wise to give in
The Devil can't win
God knows how you've been
He's seen all your sins

Take things in stride
Let Him inside
Good things will start
Open your heart

Things you once did
You no longer do
Tiger stripes change
A new creature are you

If you forgive
And choose to live
Like a wholesome host
Of the Holy Ghost

You now walk in the light
What was dark is now bright
God will keep you in sight
What He sees brings delight

~ I Keep Watch ~

Donald T. Williams

I keep watch
And hope I see

All the signs
There are to see

With my eyes
And with my mind

I keep watch
For signs divine

Some may say
"Look there is Christ"

And be fooled
By tricks so sly

But God's folk
Won't be deceived

Won't be tricked
Do not believe

False prophets
Some day appear

Christians know
The day is near

Learn a lesson
From the fig tree

When tender twigs,
You soon will see

Green tender leaves
Sprout out too

The time is near
When you see you do

There'll be false Christ's
Miracles too

You must keep watch
God has warned you
So terrible
Those days will be

So great the toll
And suffering

I keep close watch
And hope I see

All of the signs
There are to see

With open eyes
With open mind
I keep close watch
For signs divine

~ From Yonder Heights ~

Donald T. Williams

I sleep on a bed of stars
My head rest on a pillow, Mars
Space and time begin and end
In succession again and again

When the sunrise sweeps across my face,
I awaken by my Father's grace
Giving thanks to my true friend
I sing praises in the wind

A gentle breeze or gale may blow
Either way the world shall know
My life is His, and He is mine
An endless love through space and time

From yonder heights
Your Son shines bright
Filling my soul
Making me whole

I feel His spirit
His voice I hear it
Saying "Don't fear"
"The time is near"

Just hold on fast
And stay on task
For as you know
Reap what you sow

I sleep on a bed of stars
My head rest on a pillow, Mars
Space and time begin and end
In succession again and again

When the sunrise sweeps across my face,
I awaken by my Father's grace
Giving thanks to my true friend
I sing praises in the wind

A gentle breeze or gale may blow
Either way the world shall know
My life is His, and He is mine
An endless love through space and time

From yonder heights
Your snow falls white
Makes what's dark light
A wondrous sight

On bended knee
I do agree
The Lord of Lords
Is King of Kings

My life is His, and He is mine
An endless love through space and time

~ When I Pray ~

Donald T. Williams

When I pray,
I'm on my knees
I'm in the church
Or showering

I'm in a shop
Or at a show
No matter where
I'm sure He knows

When I pray,
It's from my heart
For someone else
Is how I start

With thanks to Thee
For all blessings
I vow my love
Eternally

Take to the air
My humble prayers!
How I beseech
His ears they reach!

Sound off of clouds
Softly or loud
Through atmosphere
Somehow He hears

When I pray
I may say words
Just think thoughts
No sound is heard

I transmit,
and He receives
This I think
and do believe

Take to the air
My humble prayers!
How I beseech
His ears they reach!

Sound off of clouds
Softly or loud
Through atmosphere
Somehow He hears

When I pray,
It's from my heart
For someone else
Is how I start

When I pray
I may say words
Just think thoughts
No sound is heard

I transmit,
and He receives
This I think
and do believe

~ The Cross of Christ ~
Donald T. Williams

The Cross of Christ
Is like a crossroad in life

Don't turn left
Don't turn right

Keep straight forward
Keep the prize in sight

There are so many roads before you
Which one will you use?

Even when there's just two
Which one will you choose?

Which way is much smoother?
Which route is the best?

Consider your choice
Your life's road is a test

Some roads are not to be taken
Which one will you choose?

Some roads are a gamble
Are you ready to lose?

Has your decision
Already been made for you?

Fixed predestination
There's really nothing for you to do

Some believe in luck, chance,
Or getting the right breaks

There's no belief in destiny
Or a prewritten fate

Is this
"Much Ado about Nothing?"

Signed, sealed, and delivered
Sure thing?

Has the Master Planner
Already laid things out?

He knows just where you're going
For Him, there is no doubt

Belief in Him and Trust
Is what's required of you

Let Him lead the way
Keep Faith in Him that's True

The Cross of Christ
Is like a crossroad in life

Don't turn left
Don't turn right

Keep straight forward
Keep the prize in sight

~ Resurrection ~

Donald T. Williams

Jesus died and then
Rose from the dead
Gave His mortal life
For eternal life instead

His sacrifice
Was in no way self-serving
His trust in God was profound and unswerving
His sacrifice
Was for His flock
He gave to man what man could not

On the Cross of Calvary
The Father sacrificed His Son
His loss was our victory
And Jesus is the truly, Risen One

In our lives, we as men
Will face similar tribulations and trials
We may feel abandoned,
Alone, like a parentless child

We, as lambs, must walk this earth
With its earthly and unearthly beasts
Be prepared for any test of
Love
Faith
Character
Wisdom
Strength
Generosity
Goodness
Obedience
And doubtless belief

For there is a most dark one
His lifeless heart hideously filled
With gross hatred
For all mankind
He will make you see things
Wish you were blind and without mind

Word is, he has a stencil, some
Die cast
Tattoo ink
Computer chip
Or indentifying mark
For those who bare it,
Hounds of Hell shall bark

The future for these lost souls
Is black and bleak
Make sure you don't bare it
This Mark of the Beast

Jesus died, rose, and ascended to Heaven
That's what steadfast Christians know
And believe
What if He's not the only one,
Who can rise from the depths of misery?

Each of us have in us
The power to rise from the dead
Each of us are winners in Christ
No matter what the Devil's losers said

Live, die, and rise with Jesus
It's just as it the Good Book says
Jesus is Lord and God of the living
He's not and never was into the dead

Rise and shine my fellow lambs
The Shepherd's soon to return
Anyone baring the Mark of the Beast
Stay put
Be prepared to suffer and burned

Your goose is being cooked and burned
Roasted and toasted, well beyond well done
Is this the miserable fate for you?
Are you the unread one?

You let the Good Book gather dust
Your need to read was not a must
Never opened, never schooled
You lived a long life as a fool

Were you
Selfish
Unread
Dishonest
Disloyal
Prejudice
Lustful
Lazy
Greedy
Gluttonous
Beastial
Unkind
Mean
Or downright cruel?

Jesus died and then
Rose from the dead
Gave His mortal life
For eternal life instead

Jesus offers you a way out,
A pardon you should take
Turning down His offer
Be the worst mistake you make

His sacrifice
Was in no way self-serving
His trust in God was profound and unswerving
His sacrifice
Was for His flock
He gave to man what man could not

On the Cross of Calvary
The Father sacrificed His Son
His loss was our victory
And Jesus is the truly, Risen One

P.S. Thank you Pastor Arnold Murray of the Good Shepherd
Ministry

~ So Holy ~

Donald T. Williams

So Holy is the Bible
So Holy is God's Word

It has an affect and effect on you
When spoken or unheard

Try to read it often
When you can both night and day

Read it in the morning
And when the sun has gone away

Rise and raise with it in the East
Set and sit with it in the West

Read it for pure pleasure
Read and study it as for a test

Whatever be your reason
Read through the seasons; it's the best

Why one would not read it
Is anybody's guess?

So Holy is the Bible
So Holy is God's Word

Not to take Him at it
Is foolish and absurd

Won't you be the wise one
When six trumpet sounds are heard?

Wait until the seventh trump
As forewarned in God's own Word

Don't say He did not tell you
Don't say that I can't or didn't read

When His Word is read, heard, or spoken
It's foolish for you not to heed

His Promises will not be broken
God always keeps His Word

Keeps it with the small sparrow
Keeps it with the elephant's herd

Keeps it with the minute minnow
Keeps it with the massive manatee

Keeps it with the cock crowing rooster
Keeps it with the busy bumble bee

Why? If I may ask you,
Would He not keep His Word with you?

Why would my God even say it,
If for you, His Word was not true?

Do you have an answer?
Tell us all, but with all due respect

Only God has all the answers
And it's His wisdom I respect

So Holy is the Bible
So Holy is God's Word

It has an affect and effect on you
When spoken or unheard

So Holy is the Bible
So Holy is God's Word

Not to take Him at it
Is foolish and absurd

~ *Music* ~

Donald T. Williams

I hear the sound
Of music far away

I love to hear the sound
Of music that is played

Harmony so sweet
I love to hear the sound

Songs sung in Heaven
When the rain falls down

On sunny days
I hear that music too

So comforting
The way it calms and soothes

For all my pains
Comes down unearthly balms

They are as great and sacred
As the Psalms

Do you not hear
This sound of music too?

Is it R and B?
Hymns?
Hip Hop?
Pop?
Or blue sky Blues?

For it is played
For sinners of this Earth

It has been played
From the time of our birth

Constant concert
For all who hear the call

It's for our ears
All creatures great and small

Let the music play
Sing with it everyday

It beats in time
With a true heart

It keeps the beat
Once your life has its start

And when you die,
The music does not end

It's when you die,
The "Show of Shows" begins

~ Every Day ~

Donald T. Williams

Every day is a good day
When you're alive in Jesus Christ

Everything comes naturally
No need to think twice

Ever faithful
Ever sure

He's the one you adore
And more

If to Him your life you give,
Everything's quite relative

Simple in a complex way
You straightly meander
Through your day

Straight or crooked course
You navigate

In time with God
And never late

He's the Lamb
Who knows your cares

He's the Lord
Who hears your prayers

He's the God
Who knows your fate

He's the love
Who counters hate

It's His day
For which we wait

In His time
And never late

Side with God
Don't hesitate

Prove yourself
With steadfast faith

Smooth, shaky, or slippery slope
Climb them all with trust and hope

Every day is a good day
When you're alive in Jesus Christ

Everything comes naturally
No need to think twice

Ever faithful
Ever sure

He's the one you adore
And more

~ Keep My Path Straight ~
Donald T. Williams

My God, keep my path straight
Grant me ease and comfort
In your work I attempt to do

Make my burdens
Light enough to carry

And my obstacles something
I can overcome, maneuver under,
Around, or through

Jesus Christ, my Savior
Has already paid my dues

Keep my challenges formidable,
For in Him, there is nothing I can't do

I am your foot soldier
At your beckon call
Or instantaneous command

I fight the "good fight" for you
And I hold the fort
Like The Alamo's Last Stand

General George Custard
Died in battle
Surrounded and unable
To retreat in any way

I fight the battle
'Til the last breath

Fall and rise
Right away,
Or in three day's time

Like "The Charge of the Light Brigade"
With swords clashing and
Cannon fire on all three sides
It's not for me to question
I just fight like do or die

I'm one of God's foot soldiers
Of good heart,
Brave heart,
Honor,
And noble deeds
I answer to His call
As if my God has needs

Shirk or run from battle?
There are times
When common sense must prevail
I'm battle worn and tested
Fight
With every tooth and nail

So menacing to evil
True blue
Under God's leadership,
Armor,
Cloak and veil

His enemies are my sworn enemies
I will defend,
Attack,
Assault,
Vanquish,
And decidedly prevail

My sworn oath
Is to serve God
To protect the widow and child
To do what's right
Within God's sight
To do it with a smile

My God, keep my path straight
Grant me ease and comfort
In your work I attempt to do

Make my burdens
Light enough to carry
And my obstacles
Something
I can overcome, maneuver under,
Around, or through

Jesus Christ, my Savior
Has already paid my dues

Keep my challenges formidable,
For in Him, there is nothing I can't do

~ Courtroom ~
Donald T. Williams

There's a courtroom I must face
Full of people of my race

I must stand and plead my case
Swift justice at a reasonable pace

Where I'm originally from
Only the stars above really know

Can barely trace my ancestor's footprints
Back to the cotton fields and the plantation's hoe

God will be the final Judge
Before Him I'll have to stand

Will I measure up according to Him?
Really be considered a "good" man?

Standing before the court of man,
I am like Daniel in the lion's den

Do I have a split hair's chance
They don't convict me or ask me to dance?

You see man's justice is not really
And far from blind

Not near sighted or farsighted
No such thing of any kind

It picks and chooses to see what it wants
Or doesn't want to see

What it primarily wants to see most
Is injustice for folks like you and me

Why do they have to make it so hard
For a brother to make bail?

Why does he or she have to wait months
Or even years before the courts move like crippled snails?

Why is our society
Hell bent on creating criminals,

Failing its underprivileged masses,
And building more jails?

Is this the way the greatest nation of the "free" world
Has to have its court system run?

Got us standing before judge and jury
Maybe they're the ones who need to be hung?

Countless lives laid to waste
When it's potential and productivity we crave

Hoarding the wealth of this land while the "little"
People are in need and beg

There's a courtroom and a judge
I must one day face

Stand before my God seeking His mercy and grace
Hope I'm man enough to face Him in the most Holy Place

Dignified, humbly strong,
Head bowed but standing tall

It's the biggest court date
That's facing us all

~ Reason ~

Donald T. Williams

Is there any sound
And reasonably unreasonable reason
That you will
Or will not agree with me

That Jesus Christ
Is the Risen Son
Who guarantees
Our undisputed victory?

Is there any reasonably
Valid degree of incredulous doubt
That could, would, or should prevent
You to stand, scream, and shout

That my Lord, Jesus Christ
Is my sole soul Savior
The "One" of endless power
And unending clout?

Is there any possible
Reason or explanation
Of how our Earth
Its Solar System
Galaxy
Universe
Wormhole
And Blackhole
Came into existence
And for us to come to be?

Is there any dubious
Questionable or unquestionable
Question or query

That leaves us and arrives
In conclusive results
Of improbable yet probable
Possibilities of probability?

That Jesus Christ
Is man's Savior

Who will return
To Earth
The place
of His birth

In His Father's own sweet time
Who on Judgment Day
Will pick us
Like fine, ripe fruit,
Or sweet grapes

Grown in His vineyard
And on His every vine?

Is there any sound
And reasonably unreasonable reason
That you will
Or will not agree with me

That Jesus Christ
Is the Risen Son
Who guarantees
Our undisputed victory?

~ How Can It Be? ~
Donald T. Williams

Silent prayers
Intimate thoughts I share
With my true God
Are neither coaxed
Nor prodded

Freely they flow
To Him that knows
My prayers don't whine
Or waste His time

How can it be
I'm sure of this?
I have His ear
As His witness

What I see
Is seen by Him

And what I say
Sings like a hymn

And what I do
Is not in vain

My words and acts
All praise His name

How can it be
I'm sure of this?

I turn my cheeks
And feel His kiss

I am His son
And He is my dad

I bring Him joy
And I make Him glad

How can it be
I'm sure of this?

His love fills me
And I can't resist

I eat the bread
Which is unleaven

I drink the wine
And toast to Heaven

These things I do
In remembrance of

The Son of God
Jesus Christ

I love

How can it be
I'm sure of this?

I turn my cheeks
And feel His kiss

How can it be
I'm sure of this?

His love fills me
And I can't resist.

~ Life's Gamble ~
Donald T. Williams

Lord, My God
Have mercy
And keep my enemies at bay

Lord, My God
Have influence
In the words I'm about to say

Now, the "game" is surely afoot
And "winner takes all"
Is the mind set at its roots

Life's one big gamble
All who live and die
Are obligated to play

God's House has set
The rules of play

And all players
Have absolutely no say

What you're allowed
Is free choice

What you choose
Or don't choose
Is solely up to you

Chances are
The uncertainty
Of your certain outcome

Again, boils down
To the choices made by you

More than a casual wager
When it's your soul and eternal life
That could be lost

More than a risky side bet
When the time comes
To ante up an inordinate cost

We all start out
With a clean slate
Chalk it up
With both rights and wrongs

Checks and balances
In two columns
Which one of the two
Will be the longer one?

Losers don't realize
They've already lost
Long before the "gaming" has begun

Winners are rightfully confident
Because they know
That they've already won

What's the point or thrill of a victory
When you know
There was nothing to be lost?

I'll always wager on a "sure thing"
When I work for the House
And My God is the Boss

Have you gambled lately?
Sure you know
What really is at stake?

The Devil's got a stake
In this game

But God's House
He can't
And never, ever
Break

Lord, My God
Have mercy
And keep my enemies at bay

Lord, My God
Have influence
In the words I'm about to say

Life's one big gamble
All who live and die
Are obligated to play

God's House has set
The rules of play

And all players
Have absolutely no say

~ Life With God ~
Donald T. Williams

Life with God
And life with Christ
Holy Spirit's
Eternal life

Becomes mine
I'm one of them

The faith in me
Is the faith in Him

All of this
By God's grand design

Who does not
Call Him divine?

Yes, there are
Several foolish who

Had their chance
To begin anew

Had the chance
Of the chosen few

Who realized
What they had to do

Had their place
And had their time
To live life right
And prefer the divine

Chances lost
Opportunities unclaimed

Wasted lives
Of sin and shame

The end result
Is an eternity in Hell

Brimstone's heat
And sulfur's smell

This is what
You sinful losers win

This gruesome reward
Awards your wages of sin

Chances are
You burn again
And again

Longing for
What might
Could
Would
Or
Should
Have been

Life with God
And life with Christ
Holy Spirit's
Eternal life

It's mine
I'm one of them
The faith in me
Is the faith in Him

~ All ~

Donald T. Williams

All
Within my arm's length

All
Within my grasp

All
That I could long for

All
That I could ask

He provides all these things for me
No charge to my account

Nothing is too trivial
Never too much is the amount

Why do I have it like that?
Why do I have it so good?

All
He said was to obey me
And live life as I should

Love for an enemy like a brother
Is what counts
In His eyes on the Mount

Names long ago written
In the Book of Life

Long before any ink, print,
Script, type or computer font

Giving without strings attached
Is considered a true, honest,
And charitable deed

Giving to the shoeless child

Tending to the elderly's every need

Providing the best health care
For any race of women or men

Treat benign or malignant A's to Z's
As if they were a simple nosebleed

Fill the needs of your "equal" fellow men

Because it matters to Him
How well – heeled or astronomically
Wealthy you may be

Did you see a need and fill it
Or deem "them" a lesser breed
Of God's seed?

Great wealth can burn to ashes

Fortunate ebbs and tides
Can earthquake to economic tsunamis

Inflated egos quickly deflate or burst
With the prick of a tiny but crucial
Economic linchpin

Somehow "they" underestimated its
Importance, value, necessity, or basic needs

One moment, a floral garden's beautiful,
Bountiful bouquet on display

The next moment, a dustbowl's
Turbulent, tumbling, tumble weed
Tumbles aimlessly on its way

All
Within our arms' length

All
Within our grasp

All
That we could long for

All
That we could ask

All
He said was to obey me
And live life like I've asked

All
He said was love one another
Is "loving" too hard to ask?

~ Self Reflection ~
Donald T. Williams

Get out of this slump
Get on with the pain

What's to come has to come
Like a forty day rain

You're just an instrument
You're just a tool

You can't take the blame
For what's coming so cruel

There's a time and a place
For all things you must know

Your quiver is max full
Time to draw back your bow

All targets are marked
And simply, don't stand a chance

There's no time for love
There's no chance for romance

This time is for war
This time is for hate

Jesus Christ is coming
No longer the wait

People are like animals
Animals behave as people do

Writers call that personification
Which of us or them
"Actually belong"
In a cage or zoo?

What happens to animals
Happens to people too

Death waits for both
Both Man and Kangaroo

Nothing has any meaning
How's that
For a convenient or inconvenient
Truth?

Who really killed Old Honest Abe?
Was it really an actor named Booth?

Truth and/or fiction
Mixed with timeless, honest
Spin-doctor lies
Fly and lite like flies
At an unattended picnic table

Magic bullets buzzing
About John F. Kennedy
And bang, bang
A sitting President
Or sitting duck
Carved and served
Upon the table

People and animals go to the same place
No matter the species
No matter the race

Nothing has any meaning
But, there is one truth

Jesus Christ is coming
The Risen Dead is Living Proof

Get out of this slump
Get on with the pain

What's to come has to come
Like a forty day rain

I'm just an instrument
I'm just a tool

I can't take the blame
For what's coming so cruel

For the people long suffering,
The time for comfort is now

Lift up your heads, hands, and hearts
Then prepare to bow low
To bow low down

Your King of Kings
Your Lord of Lords
Your Prince of Peace and Pasture
Your Son of God
Your Soul Savior
Your Seed of the Grand Master
Is coming

Wearing His Holy Crown
Leading an army of millions

And raining fire
All the oceans can't drown

Get on with the lumps
Yeah,
Here comes the pain

What's to come has to come
Will you now...

Praise His name?

~ The Power of One ~

Donald T. Williams

The power of One
Has risen
For those who would fall
His name is The Lord
Who Rules Over All

The First and The Last
Sum of One, only, and most
No one is like Him
There is none
Who can boast

Call His name Jesus
Confess what you shame
Repent for all sins
Justify why He came

Did He not hang
Until his last breath?
Ascend from the tomb
And defy what is death?

Live life unblemished
Live life unstained
Jesus did do it
His goodness remains

Set fine examples
Of what men and women should do
Remember the children
Look up, watch, and love you

The power of One
Is the power of light
The Son shines the way
The path which is right

Follow Him and God
To whom He has knelt
Love Him and God
Whose love He has felt

Trust Him and God
Who makes us secure
Believe Him and God
For whom we keep pure

The power of One
Is God's only Son
Do as He said
Lest innocent blood be shed

His was enough
There need be no more
The stone once rolled back
Opened Heaven's door

The power of One
Has risen
For those who would fall
His name is the Lord
Who rules over All

The First and The Last
Sum of One, only, and most
No one is like Him
There is none
Who can boast

Call His name Jesus
Confess what you shame
Repent for all sins
Justify why He came

The Spirit Made Me Do It
Difficult life lessons learned the hard way made simpler via God's way

Would have, could have, should have were all I could come up with after I finally got around to reading the Bible midway through my fifty-eighth year of life. Being a retired English teacher, I have read my share of fine novels, short stories, plays, poems and letters over the years, each with its premise, lesson or moral. But the Bible, the most important literary work of all, I had deliberately avoided. I reasoned that "not knowing" would somehow diminish my accountability for the flaws of my imperfect existence. Ignorance was almost bliss for a while.

This cop out was working just fine for me until life threw me a succession of 140 mph fast and curve balls. I got beamed something fierce, but it knocked some much needed sense into me. Yes, there was a weighty price for my knowledgeable ignorance, but I believe I know that I'm better for it. So, look at me now....spreading the "good news" in the only humble way I know how. Who would have ever thought? The Holy Spirit? Only God knows.

I do hope that you enjoy reading these verses and consider them heaven sent as I certainly do. It's the only way I can account for something or someone, God Almighty. The Spirit Made Me Do It.

About the Author

I, a baby boomer, was born in Brooklyn, NY. I lived and worked there most of my life before retiring from the New York City Department of Education in 2004. After more than three decades of loyal service, it was a relationship that I loved but which ended unexpectedly, as did the break up of my equally long marriage. The separation in both regards was equally traumatic and painful for me, to say the least.

The psychological and emotional pain of losing two things I held most dearly was the catalyst for this, and other creative endeavors which lay dormant for years. I am not sure they would have ever come into existence if it had not been for the personal loss, pain, and suffering. Before these occurrences, I lived pretty much on the edge of success and disaster, always tempting fate, pushing my luck, my body, and my family to the extreme. Daring disaster, compromising, and/or negotiating with God and the devil is pretty pompous behavior, and I confess it.

It was not until I came to realize that one's life, circumstance, and the people you love are not to be taken for granted, did I wise up. Especially when it is "you" who would ultimately be taken advantage of and summarily disposed. Everything you cherish can be gone, stripped and ripped from you, in an instant. Leaving you alone, forlorn, and forsaken. Simply tossed aside, you find yourself clicking your heels like some poor child repeating, "There's no place like home. There's no place like home." Too bad you've no home to go to now, and you can trust no one.

That's when God, Jesus Christ, and the Holy Spirit, who were always with me anyhow, said to me, Telly Savales aka Kojak style, "Donnie my boy, who loves you baby?" And just like a kid with a lollipop, I've been a sucker for the power of God and His merciful grace because it is what it is and I am what I am. If He can deliver me, and He did, hey, I've got to believe that we all have a shot at redemption and a second chance in life. But, only if you really want it. Step out in faith, believe it, and take it. Don't look back. Look forward; look up.

TO ORDER ADDITIONAL COPIES OF:

The Spirit Made Me Do It

please forward your check or money order
(plus shipping and handling) to:

Grey Spectre Enterprises, LLC
Donald T. Williams

P.O. Box 71955,
Henrico, VA 23255
(web address) www.greyspectrenterprises.com
Qty. Item Unit Cost Total
The Spirit Made Me Do It
Subtotal
Shipping
Grand
Total

SHIPPING & HANDLING:
Please add $3.00 shipping for each item ordered.
For orders placed outside of the U.S., add $6.00 shipping per item.

Ship to: Organization: _____

_____ _____ (Mr./Mrs./Ms.)_____
      Last Name   First Name

Street Address

_____, _____ _____ _____
           City   State   Zip

Phone: ( ) _____ E-mail:_____

THANK YOU FOR PLACING YOUR ORDER!!!